ON STARS
N·O·T
FALLING

SCOTT
SHALLENBARGER

Available at Amazon and other retailers

You gain strength, courage, and confidence by every experience in which you really stop to look fear in the face. You are able to say to yourself, 'I lived through this horror. I can take the next thing that comes along.'

—*Eleanor Roosevelt*

"It's like singing on a boat during a terrible storm at sea.
You can't stop the raging storm;
but singing can change the hearts and spirits of the people who are together on that ship."

—*Anne Lamott*

THIS PLAY IS DEDICATED TO THE WOMEN
WHO TAUGHT ME COURAGE:

Connie Bacon, Nancy Ernst, and Sandra Zielinski.

AND IN LOVING GRATITUDE TO:

*Brad Burke, Tim Conway, Robert Ernst, Pauline Dessler,
and Jan Rubin.*

A SPECIAL THANKS TO:

*All the actors who shaped On Stars Not Falling with their
creative contributions.*

MAY THE PLAY ENCOURAGE, GUIDE,
AND INSPIRE:

Riley and Parker

Caution

Characters

LIZ, *21, once an aspiring teacher*

JAKE, *21, once an aspiring teacher*

KALI, *21, once an aspiring painter*

MOLLY, *20, once an aspiring fashion designer*

JIMI, *20, an aspiring social worker*

WINGS, *20, once an aspiring filmmaker*

TY, *20, once an aspiring filmmaker*

Setting

Autumn.

Today.

The rooftop of a Chicago three-flat: There is a skylight; a battered screen door up left; a garden table and three chairs stage right; and a wooden bench with potters on each side down left. The top of a fire escape is above the back ledge. Party decorations, lit candles, and Christmas lights create a festive look. Electrical poles with wires rise above and beyond the rooftop finalizing the urban landscape.

On Stars Not Falling

Lights rise on Liz wearing gardening gloves and pruning a plant. She looks up to the stars. After a few moments, Jake enters from behind the skylight. He carries a large duffle bag. He takes a few steps towards LIZ; he hears footsteps and hides again. Kali enters with urgency.

KALI
The great mystery is solved.

LIZ
I went to the store for more beer.

KALI

An hour ago; and you weren't supposed to see my big set-up until after dinner.

LIZ

You've outdone yourself. Thanks.

KALI

What's the matter?

LIZ

Nothing.

KALI

You're pruning plants on your birthday.

LIZ

It's dying.

KALI

Just like the party downstairs. Ty and I had one of our fights in front of everyone; stopped the place cold.

LIZ

What happened?

KALI

He started doing these Shakespeare soliloquies he memorized for "the entertainment." I told him music was a better idea but he didn't listen.

LIZ

You should have turned on music. Loud.

KALI

I did. He jumped on the couch and did Romeo's balcony speech louder. I told him to get off the furniture and he accused me of turning into my mother which I'm not but he knows it's my biggest fear so I said, "Fine, you don't get off the couch, we don't have sex for a week."

LIZ

That got him down.

KALI

Fat chance. He said I was sending the whole feminist movement back thirty years by using sex as a weapon. I said if sex were a weapon you and your smaller than Rhode Island M-16 would've single handedly lost both world wars. He jumps off the couch, calls me a name I shan't lower myself to repeat, flies into the bathroom
and slams the door. I feel fat. Do I look fat?

LIZ

You don't look fat.

KALI

I feel fat. Anyway, he said he won't come out until I publicly apologize which I have no intention of doing in this or any other lifetime. So, it's up to you my patron saint of good cheer: Come rejuvenate the party or face the fact that we're never going to use our bathroom again.

LIZ

I'll come in soon.

KALI

Soon does not easy access to the toilet make. Tell me.

LIZ
I'm fine.

KALI
Tell me.

LIZ
I want to be alone for a few minutes. That's all.

Kali crosses and begins to take off Liz's gardening gloves.

KALI
Not on your birthday, pal. We're all here for --oh god! What is this?

LIZ
Dog blood. *(They hold a look)* On my way back from the store a car hit this dog and drove off. I scooped her off the road. I don't know why.

KALI
Are you ok?

LIZ
It was just a dog.

During the following, Kali gets the watering can. She cleans Liz's hand.

KALI
I don't buy the unaffected act.

LIZ
Do you know how the Nazi's trained the Hitler Youth to be killing machines?

KALI

(After a beat) You need a beer.

LIZ

I'm serious, Kal. Do you know?

KALI

Yeah, for six hours they put 'em in a small room with Justin Bieber.*
*(*Insert any current pop culture band lending itself to this comic moment.*)*

LIZ

I read this the other day. During their indoctrination, they gave them all puppies-- this is documented—they told the Hitler Youth their first order was to take care of these puppies: Feed them, train them, love them. 6 months later they call all the boys in and say "Now, here's your second order: Break your puppy's neck." And they did it. They had to. Who would get close to anything that you were going to kill again, right?

KALI

Let's go in.

LIZ

After I put the dog in the grass I looked up and did the whole wish on a star thing. I was bawling about some puppy I didn't even know and I wished I never learned to care so that I could navigate through all this crap with more...God, Kali. I am sick of crying. Isn't five months long enough?

KALI

(She gently takes Liz's hand)
Come down in ten minutes. *(She crosses to the door and stops)* Oh! Molly brought a new guy.

LIZ
Is he cute?

KALI
You'll have to see for yourself. All right, I'm off like a prom dress. *(She exits)*

LIZ looks back to the stars. She sees a constellation and is drawn down stage, looking at it. JAKE reappears. He remains silent for a few moments.

JAKE
Happy Birthday. *(Beat)* I knew Kal would throw you one of her famous parties.

Pause—they regard one another.

You're shocked.

LIZ
I wasn't expecting you.

JAKE
Of course not.

LIZ
How did you get up here?

JAKE
Fire escape—right before you came out.

LIZ
You hid from me.

JAKE
I don't know how to start.

LIZ
Start what?

JAKE
Oh! *(He reaches into his pocket and pulls out a gemstone)* This is for you.
I saw that look! "He went to Colorado and all I get is a *rock* for my birth-day?!" But, no worries, it's a gemstone. *(he holds it up in the moonlight)*
Blue Topaz. I found it hiking. Look how it shines. It's supposed to have healing powers, or something. *(He puts it in her hands)*

LIZ
You should keep it.

JAKE
I want you to have it.

LIZ
You should keep it.

JAKE
Okay: Say it.

LIZ
Say what?

JAKE
What you're thinking.

LIZ

I'm not—

JAKE

Thinking it?

LIZ

What?

JAKE

Say it: Jake, you were....

LIZ

I don't know --

JAKE

Say it!

LIZ

What?

JAKE

What you're thinking, what you're *feeling*: Jake, you were...

LIZ

Selfish! You ran out on me you selfish bastard!

JAKE

(Coaching her)

And "Fuck you, Jake."

LIZ
And Fuck You!

JAKE
I was selfish. And I'm sorry.

(She embraces him.)

LIZ
Thank you.

JAKE
For what?

LIZ
For saying that; I needed to hear that.

JAKE
I want to tell them the truth, Lizzie.

LIZ
What?

JAKE
I want to tell them.

LIZ
We had an agreement, Jake

JAKE
I figured some stuff out.

LIZ

No.

JAKE

Look-

LIZ

How dare you.

JAKE

Hear me out.

LIZ

I've spent the last 5 months alone. Now, you waltz in and—

JAKE

Keeping quiet's what started the whole thing.

LIZ

I refuse to have this conversation. (*She crosses to the bag of groceries and retrieves a bag of pretzels*) We are going to pretend you never brought this up. Here. Eat.

Jake hits the bag of pretzels and they smash against the back wall of the porch. He sits. Liz picks up the pretzel bag.

LIZ

I turned 21 today. The final threshold. I have no intention of going back.

Liz cleans-up the pretzels during the following. When she's finished cleaning she sits at a distance.

JAKE

I wish you could have seen Colorado with me. *The mountains!* You can't believe how great they are--it was like the air was erasing all the shit in my head and for the first time in months I noticed things outside myself again. I swear, Lizzie, it was like that place, everything working together in harmony, you know, helped me see the trees, the flowers, the sky like I'd never seen them before. The miracle of it--the sudden understanding that the world has been turning for all time: Sunrise, sunset no matter what happens in between. *It survives.* And there I was: The guy who ran away. I don't think you can cross the next threshold until you're real with the past, Lizzie. You can *think* you've moved on, talk yourself into it, but one day the past creeps back in and you realize you've been running in circles. That's what I figured out.

LIZ

If we tell them, Jake, they'll never forgive us. *(beat)* Actually, I'll be the one they feel sorry for. They'll hate you. They'll hate Michael. I don't want that. I don't have any other family.

JAKE

I'll risk that to--

LIZ

Haven't you hurt me enough?

JAKE

I'm going to tell them with or without you.

LIZ

(Putting the rock in his hand)
If you do, I'll never speak to you again.

VOICES
(Singing off-stage)
"Happy Birthday to you/Happy Birthday to you...(cont.)"

Molly, Kali, and Jimi enter. They are wearing party hats, leis, etc. Jimi carries an Ipod and portable speakers. Wings accompanies the song with a kazoo and Kali holds two bottles of champagne. At the end of the song, Wings goes to his knees and blows the kazoo in a final, celebratory blast. Jake crosses into their view.

JAKE
Hi, everybody.

MOLLY
Oh my god! *(She runs and embraces him)*
Where'd you go? What was it like? And why the hell didn't you write?

JAKE
Lots of places. Colorado, Arizona--it was amazing.

MOLLY
What happened?

JAKE
I have a lot to tell you guys.

MOLLY
Well, tell. Tell!

LIS
Molly...introductions.

MOLLY
Ohmigod! Jake, Liz, this is Jimi; Psychology major at Columbia.

JAKE
Very cool. How'd you guys hook up?

MOLLY/JIMI
We—*(they laugh at themselves)*

MOLLY
We ran into each other at the grocery store—literally.

JIMI
Organic Food Aisle.

KALI
Love at first tofu.

JIMI
I reached for the lentils—

MOLLY
I came around the corner—

JIMI
And *(they clap their hands)*—

JIMI/MOLLY
The rest is history.

MOLLY

Doesn't he have the cutest little dimples on the planet--*(to Jimi)* ...I'm sorry, I didn't mean, oh, hells bells. Did I embarrass you? I'm sorry.

ALL *(save Jimi)*

Stop apologizing, Mol.

MOLLY

Oh, rats, I, OK.....Jimi, this is Liz--

JIMI

Hi.

LIZ

Nice dimples.

MOLLY

And this is Jake, our friend who traveled out west all summer.

JAKE

Nice to meet, ya. I can't believe someone's actually putting up with her.

MOLLY

Hey!

JAKE

Hey!

Jake tickles her or some other variation of affectionate play. Everyone laughs.

KALI

Welcome home Scrappy. So, did'ya get laid out there in the wild, wild west?

JAKE

Nope.

KALI

Liar. Who'dya hook up with?

JAKE

Just the desert, moon, and stars.

KALI

Great: You left a man and came back a poet. Somebody get this Sally a beer. We've gotta butch him up again.

WINGS

Actually, Native Americans believe—

KALI

No Native American sayings until after midnight. We can't subject Jimi to philosophy until we're all drunk.

WINGS

It's not a saying. It's a belief.

KALI

Just because you're 10% Navajo—

WINGS

Shawnee.

WINGS/MOLLY/JAKE/LIZ
25% Shawnee.

KALI
Doesn't mean we should bore the guest.

JIMI
Actually, I'd like to hear it. I love that stuff.

KALI
Drink up troops. It's going to be a long night.
(*She gives Molly, Jimi, Liz, and Jake each a beer during the following*)

WINGS
Native Americans believe in "spirit warriors." You said Jake left a man and came back a poet.

KALI
I was joking. Scrappy over there's way too sexy to ever lose his man card.

WINGS
But a spirit warrior is both at once: Strong-Soft-Man.

KALI
I prefer my men hard.

MOLLY
Kali!

KALI
You do, too. Don't deny it.

Jake crosses to Wings. They hug.

16

JAKE
Man, I missed you, Wings.

WINGS
I missed you, too.

KALI
Okay, to be fair, Jimi, Wings cured my insomnia with a Native American healing ritual.

LIZ/MOLLY/JAKE
You never had insomnia.

KALI
I feel fat. Do I look fat?

LIZ/MOLLY/JAKE
You don't look fat.

KALI
Shit. I did it again.

MOLLY
What?

KALI
Scared the guest. Look at his face.

JIMI
No, I'm just—

JAKE
Looking for a crucifix in case she comes closer?

KALI
Ass.

JIMI
Is that a family name?

KALI
Yes, Jake comes from a long line of Asses.

JIMI
(laughing) No. His. *(to Wings)* Yours. Is it a Native American--

JAKE
Wings is a nickname we gave him in college.

MOLLY
Tell the story, Jake.

JAKE
Go ahead.

MOLLY
You tell it better.

JAKE
Well, the first day of our freshman year--

MOLLY
None of us knew each other yet--

JAKE
Word got out that there was this guy on the 14th floor of the dorm—

MOLLY
Standing on the window ledge--

JAKE/MOLLY
Naked.

JIMI
No way.

JAKE
As a blue jay.

WINGS
I didn't think people could see me so high up.

MOLLY
And the sun was setting. I remember the police saying they didn't want you out there in the dark.

WINGS
They thought I wanted to jump. I just liked the way it felt.

JAKE
Then he stretched his arms out. You could feel everyone holding their breath, looking up, waiting for this guy to fly.

JIMI
Wings. Nice.

LIZ
Then you went back inside.

WINGS
I had to go to the bathroom.

They laugh

LIZ
Speaking of which, I'll get Ty. Come with me, Jake.

JAKE
He's here?

KALI
He's pouting in de bano.

MOLLY
They fought.

KALI
He lost.

WINGS
It wasn't pretty.

LIZ
Come on, let's surprise him.

MOLLY
I can't wait to see his face. What a great night! I love this night. I love you guys. I'm being a big cheese ball but I don't care. *(She kisses Jimi on the cheek)*   Thanks for coming. Oh, fuck. *(to Jimi)* Was that too much? Am I being too much? Shit-fuck-fuck. *(Jimi takes her hand. They smile at one another)*

LIZ
(Taking Jake's hand) We'll be back with Ty.

KALI
Careful, he bites.

WINGS
As if you'd want it any other way.

KALI
Go build a casino.

JAKE
(Makes a "buzzer" sound)
Ehhh! Stereotype!

KALI
If the moccasin fits....

MOLLY
Kal!

JAKE
Ehh!

KALI
You're right. Forgive me Shaman, oh my Shaman.

WINGS
On one condition...

KALI
Anything.

WINGS
Truth or Dare?

KALI
Dare, of course.

WINGS
Hug me.

KALI
No.

WINGS
Hug me.

KALI
I'm not a sap and you know it.

WINGS
You said "dare."

KALI
I reject the game.

WINGS
I reject your apology.

(Kali hugs Wings. Then, she turns out front and speaks as if she's addressing a class)

KALI
And from that moment forward, they called it Thanksgiving.

LIZ
Come on, Jake.

MOLLY
Let's all go surprise Ty!

JAKE
Actually, I need to talk to all of you.

LIZ
Not now.

JAKE
There's a reason I came back.

LIZ
For my birthday, they know. Let's get Ty.

JAKE
I want to talk to them.

KALI
What's up with you two?

(*Ty enters with a primal scream, spraying silly string at everyone.*)

ALL
Ty! Knock it off. Asshole! etc.

TY

O villainy! Ho! Let the door be locked,
Treachery, seek it out.
Exchange forgiveness with me noble Hamlet;
Mine and my father's death come not upon thee,
Nor thine on me.
(He points the can of silly string at himself and changes character.)
Heaven make thee free of it, Laertes!
I follow thee!
(He blasts himself with silly string and executes a dramatic death.)
I am dead, Horatio.

JAKE

And flights of angels sing thee to thy rest.

TY

Jake! You be alive!

Ty pulls Jake to the ground and they wrestle. After, they hug.

KALI

No performances tonight. You promised.

TY

All great poets live their art.

KALI

Living their lives every once in awhile probably didn't hurt.

TY

(Grabbing a chair, he sits Kali in it)

Illustrious members of the jury, exhibit A: charming on the outside, yes, but!, can it be? A murderer! A cold-blooded killer of passionate ideas. Give her the chair! *(He strikes a pose.)* Exhibit B: An artist. A poet. An enlightened spirit who--

KALI
Likes to feel his tongue flap in the breeze,

TY
Hypocrite!

KALI
Poser!

TY
Satan!

KALI
(After a beat)
Republican!

Ty feigns a knife to the heart and collapses to the floor.

Show over. Time for munchies!

They move about distributing food, finding a place to sit.

JAKE
So, Jimi, how's good ole Columbia?

JIMI

Chicago's great. I never thought I'd like living in the city.

JAKE

There's nothing like going out on lakeshore drive--skyline on one side, beach on the other.

LIZ

Wait 'til you see Michigan Avenue at Christmas.

TY

Yeah, it's a gas if you don't get trampled to death by the carriage horses. Very festive.

JAKE

I love this city; especially in summer.

JIMI

Why'd you leave?

PAUSE

KALI

Last May a good friend of ours died.

JAKE

I needed time away; sort things out.

JIMI

Sure.

KALI

You didn't tell Jimi about Michael?

MOLLY

I wanted him to meet all of you first. Sorry.

KALI/TY

Stop apologizing, Mol.

KALI

He died of a brain hemorrhage. He's from...He *was* from Chicago, so he lived at home instead of in the dorm like the rest of us. Anyway, his parents found him in his room one morning when he didn't get up for class.

TY

Alderman Thompson and his trophy wife.

JIMI

His dad's a politician?

MOLLY

A prominent one.

KALI/TY

A prominent asshole.

MOLLY

None of us were allowed at the funeral.

JIMI

Why?

KALI

Family only. What bullshit. We were his family.

TY

It was all over the papers—big media spectacle.

WINGS

And the people who knew him best said goodbye watching a 10 second news clip.

JAKE

There's something I want to say about Michael.

LIZ

Wait. Let me. I now what you're going to say and I'd like to say it.

JAKE

Really?

LIZ

I have that right, don't I? *(to Jimi)* Michael and I were engaged.

JIMI

I'm sorry for your loss.

JAKE

Are you sure you don't want me to—

LIZ

Please don't interrupt. I want to start at the beginning. Jimi, the day we saw Wings on top of the building the crowd left after he went back in his room. But for some reason the six of us stayed.

TY
Remember, we didn't know each other yet.

KALI
Let her tell the story.

TY
Go ahead, Liz.

LIZ
And after the cops talked to him—

TY
And chastised him for being a bad boy, attention seeker.

WINGS
I didn't know anyone could see me. I just liked the way it felt.

TY
Right.

KALI
Ty.

TY
Sorry. Go ahead Liz.

LIZ
Wings walks out of the building like nothing bizarre happened. And we all sort of look at each other and Michael throws his arm around Wings like he's known him his whole life and says "You guys wanna go get pizza?" So we did.

MOLLY

We hung out the next night too.

KALI

We went to the beach.

MOLLY

We made a campfire.

TY

We got kicked out by the police.

LIZ

We've been together ever since. He knew we were meant to be a family. And he had the gift to lift us up—to make us all feel special.

WINGS

There is a Native American saying: I want to know if you can see beauty in the world even when it's not a pretty day. Michael could.

TY

And he was crazy! Good crazy, you know? He planned an entire camping trip for us last fall. When we got there he had us all wade into the lake —and he had planned this, you know—like, this was his big surprise for us-- and he started trickling water over our heads saying, "Now all the crap of civilized life is washed away. Welcome to new things."

WINGS

Not "new things." "Welcome to beautiful things."

TY

Beautiful things.

WINGS

Then we lay down on the sand to dry. I looked up at the clouds and thought: "I'm home."

KALI

Michael insisted we look at the stars every night and memorize the constellations. I tried to tell him a star was a star --not to mention the fact

most of them are burnt out by the time we see them--but he didn't care. And he loved falling stars, the sap. He stayed up all night waiting and when he finally saw one he screamed, "Never was there a more glorious descent!" I said "descent this" and threw a flashlight at him for waking us up.

JAKE

All that is true, he was amazing, but—

LIZ

(simply)

I haven't made my point, yet.

JAKE

Go ahead.

LIZ

How many of you think of Michael every day?

TY

Without question.

MOLLY

I don't know what I'd do if I couldn't picture his smile to get through a hard time.

KALI

More than once a day; I miss his optimism.

LIZ

Me, too.

WINGS

His spirit walks with me. *(touching his heart)* Right here.

JIMI

He sounds like an amazing guy.

TY

Sometimes, just picturing his face....

He begins to tear up. Kali touches his hand.

LIZ

(to Jake) Is that what you were going to say?

Short Pause

JAKE

No.

LIZ

Oh. Sorry. Go ahead then.

They regard one another.

MOLLY
What were you going to say, Jake?

JAKE
Nothing.

KALI
Jake's right! Memory Lane closed! Who else wants a drink? *(Pulling a small, crushed velvet bag out of the cooler)* What the hell is this?

TY
                    (Leaping to his feet)
How weird! What could it be?

KALI
You planned this.

TY
                    (Taking the bag from her)
Everybody, close your eyes and stick out your hands! You won't be sorry.

(Out of the bag he retrieves a handful of round, purple beads.)

KALI
This better be good.

TY
Trust me.

KALI
Said Brutus to Caesar.

TY

(*He places a bead in each person's outstretched hand*) Once it's in your hand, make a fist. Squeeze tight. And...listen(beat) What do you hear?

JIMI

Cars in the distance—

TY

No! Not to the sounds, you know, out there, but from (he whispers) *the beads*. Hold it to your ear. Feel it vibrating.

KALI

What the fuck—

TY

Close your eyes! Let them talk to you. WHAT ARE THEY SAYING?

JAKE

Let my people go?

TY

You're not listening.

LIZ

Enlighten us.

TY

Remember last week when the woman jumped off the top of the Ferris wheel at Navy Pier and committed suicide? I was there.She hit the ground. She had on a Mardi Gras necklace. When everyone else ran to *her*—I scooped up the rolling beads. The beads were there. They know why she did it. They felt her as she fell. LISTEN TO THEM AND DISCOVER THE MYSTERY!

KALI
Ty?

TY
Yes?

KALI
You didn't actually see it. Did you?

TY
Yeah, I--

KALI
Ty?

TY
Not really. But I turned the corner just as she hit the ground. I saw the--

KALI
Ty?

TY
I was at the end of the pier and heard all the noise. *Then* I went running and saw--

KALI
Ty?

TY

I was on my way to Navy Pier and heard it on the radio. When I got there I saw--

KALI

Ty?

TY

Yesterday, a homeless guy sold me the beads and told me the story.

ALL

Ad-lib; they throw the beads at him, etc.

JIMI

Yet the question remains: Why did she jump off the Ferris Wheel? You know what I wonder—if, as she stepped off—just as she's in mid-air, the point of no return—she says to herself, "I don't want this. I want to go back." That haunts me: that moment when someone jumps or swallows the pills—not just has them in their mouth but actually swallows—

MOLLY

Or when the actual trigger is pulled—

JIMI

Exactly, what if in that flash of a millisecond, there's *regret*; a wanting to go back: To live. But you know in the same moment that life is no longer possible and your brain, can it possibly compute the realization? Or is there so much adrenaline rushing through the body when an act of suicide is happening that the person only has a sense of the present moment and no sense of past or future? Like when I went skydiving.

KALI
Couldn't pay me!

JIMI
Here's my point: When you skydive, you're on the edge of the plane ready to drop and you know that if you cross that threshold—*if you do*-- you'll be a changed person. There was this one woman who got all the way up there—13,000 feet—and freaked out—refused to jump. Can you imagine the plane ride back and sitting there—knowing you didn't do it after coming so close? How you'd feel about yourself? But I did it. I closed my eyes and just....fell out of the plane... through the sky, clouds, the air rushing past you...*through* you—there's suddenly no *thinking*—just...*experiencing.* After I landed, I had never felt so... cleansed...so, connected to everything.

KALI
So, you're saying, what if the Navy Pier woman wanted the same feeling so desperately she was willing to give up everything else to get it?

JIMI
Exactly.

MOLLY
Everyone says suicide is the weakest act. What if it's the strongest?

KALI
What?

MOLLY
It probably takes a lot of strength to overcome our instinct for survival.

JAKE
I disagree.

MOLLY
 I'm sorry. That was stupid.

TY/KALI.
Stop apologizing.

MOLLY
I'm sorry. Oh. Sor—Ok. I'm working on it.

TY
How 'bout this? One could argue that suicide brings you closer to God in that you have given up your human attachment to the earth. What do you think, Liz?

LIZ
This is depressing.

TY
But fascinating.

LIZ
The "Art of Suicide" is not my favorite party game.

TY
Come, on—

LIZ
I'd prefer to kick back and enjoy a beer on my birthday.

JAKE
Enjoy or escape?

LIZ
Shut-up, Jake.

KALI
What's going on with you two?

TY
I think the suicide thing is interesting. I mean --

LIZ
It's tasteless.

TY
What crawled up your ass?

LIZ
You're using some woman's tragedy for your entertainment.

TY
We're having a conversation.

LIZ
It's vulgar.

TY
It's philosophical debate.

LIZ
Yeah, yeah.

TY

"Yeah, yeah?" What? You say "yeah, yeah" To Shakespeare? "To be or not to be?" Suicide has always inspired--

LIZ

Philosophical Debate?

TY

Yeah.

LIZ

Is that a euphemism?

TY

For what?

LIZ

For: "I can exploit people's suffering any time I want, as long as I get off on the sound of my own voice." Grow up, Ty.

TY

Chill out!

KALI

Ladies and gentleman it is time to do what my parents taught me so expertly to do in this situation: Let's sweep the tension under the carpet, pretend it doesn't exist...and drink. Ty, music.

TY

You got it! Jimi, can I play your Ipod?

JIMI
Yep. Check out the cheesy 70's playlist.

KALI
Mol, help me with the drinks. I swear, if I have to carry these alone I'll get another hernia.

TY/WINGS/MOLLY/LIZ
You never had a hernia.

KALI
I feel fat. Do I look fat?

TY/WINGS/MOLLY/LIZ
You don't look fat.

Music plays. They all gather to work on the drinks. LIZ approaches Jake down stage.

LIZ
Listen to me.

JAKE
I'll do it alone if I have to.

LIZ
Let them remember him like they remember him.

JAKE
Like *you* want to remember him?

LIZ

Like we *agreed* to remember him.

TY

Jake! *(He tosses him a baseball. Jake catches it.)* Hey-hey. The boy's still got it.

JIMI

You play?

JAKE

High school. You?

JIMI

Little League. I sucked. The one time I saw my dad smile was when I made my only catch. I never had the heart to tell him I just stuck up my glove and prayed.

JAKE

God was listening.

JIMI

There's a first time for everything.

KALI

Gather, gather, it's toastin' time! *(Kali raises her glass and steps onto a chair)* Happy Birthday to...sorry this is hard...Happy Birthday to...the biggest fat ass I know!

MOLLY

My turn! *(She and Kali change places. Molly lifts her glass.)* To...

TY
What?

MOLLY
Look at us: Together again.

LIZ
Cheers.

KALI
Down the hatch.

WINGS
To Millie.

ALL
Who?

WINGS
On my last trip I met Millie and her husband. They were close to eighty years old and real religious. New borns.

KALI
You mean born again, right? Born again Christians?

WINGS
Yeah, new borns. And they were skinny dipping in the river.

KALI
An image I could've done without.

WINGS
I stripped and joined 'em.

KALI
(to Molly)
Shove me over the ledge.

WINGS
And then Millie's teeth fell out and floated down the river but she didn't know 'cause she was ankle deep in the water screaming "Hallelujah." So her husband ran up and down the river looking for the teeth. *(He takes a drink and smiles.)*

TY
And?

WINGS
No and.

LIZ
There's no more?

WINGS
Nope.

MOLLY
Did she find the teeth?

WINGS
There's a Native American saying:

KALI
Of course there is.

MOLLY
Shh.

WINGS
"I want to know if you can let ecstasy fill you to the tip of your fingers and your toes without remembering the limitations of being human."

TY
To Millie!

MOLLY/JIMI
To Millie!

KALI
Any more toasts? Jake?

JAKE
To getting a job and moving back to Chicago.

MOLLY
What?

JAKE
I'm home for good.

TY
What's the new gig?

JAKE

Well...there's this place on the south side, a community center for street kids who need a place to hang out. Anyway, I went over there earlier today and got hired to coach basketball.

KALI

You don't know anything about Basketball.

JAKE

True—but they don't care. They just want role models for these kids who don't have any. I start Monday.

MOLLY

To Jake!

They ad-lib responses: "Congrats!" "All Right!" Etc.

KALI

I don't know, Scrappy: I can't picture you in those little shorts grunting under a basket and scratching your balls.

TY

I can picture him scratching his balls.
(They all look at him)
Just sayin'.

JAKE

So what're you guys gonna do?

KALI

What do you mean?

JAKE
I mean when we dropped out of school we said we wouldn't let ourselves vegetate.

KALI
I'm happy doing what I'm doing.

JAKE
Waiting tables?

KALI
For now.

JAKE
Have you been painting?

KALI
Not a stroke.

JAKE
So you're going to serve porkchops 'til you're sixty?

KALI
What's with the third degree?

JAKE
What about you, Mol?

MOLLY
I've been at the store long enough to get commission.

JAKE
Are you happy?

KALI
It's not about happy. It's about surviving.

JAKE
Give me a break.

KALI
Ask anyone who works a menial job.

JAKE
Ty?

TY
Starbucks gives us a free pound of coffee every week.

JAKE
You and Wings were going to be the next great filmmakers. What happened?

TY
Reality happened.

JAKE
So you've accepted it? That's that?

KALI
Let's concentrate on important things--like this!

(She pops open a fresh bottle of champagne. Everyone cheers.)

JAKE
So that's it, huh?

KALI
Get the bug out of your butt and party!

JAKE
You'd rather sell burgers than--

MOLLY
You're being too serious, Jake.

JAKE
Too serious?

LIZ
I want to enjoy my party.

JAKE
What about teaching? We couldn't wait to be teachers.

LIZ
I don't want to.

JAKE
It's all you ever talked about.

LIZ
Exactly. Past tense.

Ty has put on new music.

TY
Let's Party!

They dance. Jake does not participate.

MOLLY
Come on, Jake!
Molly grabs his arm but he stands his ground.. The celebration continues--specifics to be determined in rehearsal--but most activity should include trying to physically engage Jake in the playfulness. It builds until finally Jake breaks away from the group, crosses to the stereo, and slams his hand on it--effectively stopping the music.

JAKE
Jesus!

KALI
What's with you?

JAKE
Everyone's dancing and acting like everything's okay--like nothing's changed!

MOLLY
It's us, Jake.

JAKE
Us? I don't know us anymore.

KALI
What the hell is eating you?

LIZ
We're fine.

JAKE
Fine? Name one person here who's fine. Raise your hands! Who's fine?

LIZ
We're all fine!

Jake picks up a half-empty glass and stands on the chair.

JAKE
To us! Who once dreamed it big! To us! Who have talent but never use it! To us! Pissing everything away but dancing like it doesn't matter. But don't worry. Everything's fine!
He throws the glass to the ground. With a fierce turn, he exits. LIZ follows him out.

PAUSE

KALI
Kitchen duty. Ty, Wings, help me out. Asthma, you know.

TY/WINGS
You never had asthma.

KALI
Whatever. Let's make like a baby and head out.

They exit.

JIMI

Up here it feels like the whole city is asleep.

MOLLY

I should have told you about Michael. I'm sorry.

JIMI

Is that why you all left school?

MOLLY

(Crosses to her purse and pulls out a picture)

We sat around the night of his funeral-- no one talked--and then Ty broke the silence and said "If life can be this random, what's the point?" We all decided together, right then and there to drop out. It seems strange now, but then we were so--I'm sorry. I'm rambling. *(She hands him the picture)* This is Michael.

JIMI

Did he always wear clothes that were too big for him?

MOLLY

(Laughing)

No. I took this on Parent's Weekend. My parents decided not to come so Michael goes to a resale shop, buys this crazy suit that's too big, and shows up at my door with flowers. He knocks and yells at the top of his lungs: "Daddy's here! "Where's my little girl? We spent the whole day together.

JIMI

I wish I could have known him.

MOLLY
He was worth knowing.

JIMI
I want to tell you something I've never told anyone. But before I do, I want you to know why I want to tell you. I can't sleep at night because of it and if I don't say it out loud I'm afraid I'll die hugging my pillow like a life preserver, because that's what I do when I can't fall asleep, I hug my pillow and pretend I'm floating on the ocean--which is something I read you're supposed to do if you can't fall asleep--but if I die because of sleep deprivation-- because I won't be able to sleep until I tell you--I don't want my friends and family to remember me as the guy who died hugging his pillow. *(beat)* So I should tell you. Look.

He lifts his shirt and reveals his stomach. We can see crosshatches of pink scars.

MOLLY
Oh my god.

JIMI
I was a cutter. In high school.

MOLLY
Jimi....

JIMI
There was a lot pain for a lot of reasons that don't matter now—

MOLLY
They do matter.

JIMI

They don't...they do, but not the way they mattered before—when all the emotional crap had this crazy power over me. I cut to relieve it all, you know to, like, convince myself I was in control of something. Anything. But it was a quick fix that fixed nothing.

MOLLY

These are wider than a razor blade.

JIMI

Scissors from my mom's sewing basket.

MOLLY gently touches the scars. Jimi closes his eyes for a moment and experiences the touch.

No one's ever done that before.

MOLLY

 I'm sorry. I shouldn't have—

JIMI

No, I didn't show you to get your sympathy. I wanted you to know so if you saw them later—I'm not suggesting anything, like I expect anything that would entail having my shirt off--but, like, if you saw them later, in the future, for whatever reason, you wouldn't think I was hiding something. I don't want to hide anything from you because—

MOLLY

How do you survive something like that?

JIMI

Lots of hours with a great therapist. When I stopped she gave me this bracelet so I would always remember--my god you have beautiful eyes--

MOLLY
What?

JIMI
You have stunning eyes.

MOLLY
No—

JIMI
You do.

MOLLY
No, so you can always remember what?

JIMI
What?

MOLLY
The bracelet.

JIMI
That I have the strength to make it through whatever gets thrown at me. Can I tell you the "why" now? Before I burst?

MOLLY
I bet they're wondering where we are. Maybe we should—

JIMI
I love you.

MOLLY
Oh.

Short, painful pause

JIMI
Oh.

JIMI pulls a piece of paper from his pocket. He reads:

> When will God bring us together, we,
> Two separate, wandering ships,
> Battered by the furious sea.
> Together we could fill our sails with
> Wonder, Love,
> And tame the raging storm.

He hands it to her. She holds it but looks away

I wrote it for you. *(beat)* Say something.

MOLLY
What?

JIMI
Anything. *(beat)* Maybe I should go.

MOLLY
I used to write poetry, when I was in high school, you know, adolescent angst, trauma drama, DIARY, whatever, I used to sing, choir, you know, art geek, dyed my hair black, never mind, forget it, rambling!

JIMI
Why'd you stop?

MOLLY
I hate when I ramble.

JIMI
"Used to" write and sing? Why'd you stop?

MOLLY
My mother thought they were stupid.

JIMI
And you listened to her.

Molly suddenly starts laughing.

JIMI
What?

MOLLY
I just remembered—*(a new burst of laughter)*

JIMI
What?

MOLLY
I danced in my room to Barry Manilow songs. 7ᵗʰ grade: I dreamed of being a Barry Manilow back-up singer. Shit. Fuck. You think I'm a dork. Shit-fuck. Okay, time to go in. La-dee-da. *(Jimi crosses to the stereo)* What're you doing?

JIMI
Don't look.

MOLLY
What are you—

JIMI
Nothing. Don't look.

MOLLY
Jimi!

Suddenly, music starts. Barry Manilow's "Copacabana." Jimi speaks to an imaginary audience.

JIMI
Ladies and Gentlemen, please welcome the voice behind the magic! *(He presents Molly, she laughs.)* Miss Molly, please! There are thousands of fans waiting to see you. They're not here for Barry--they've never been here for Barry--It's always been for you. Do you hear what I'm saying? They want you!

MOLLY
Hit it boys!

They sing along and animate the story of Tony and Lola--they dance a mock tango during the chorus. At some point, Jimi stops and looks into her eyes. They discover one another. Molly stops. They move toward one another slowly. Jimi pulls her into him and kisses her. Molly pulls away, crosses, and turns off the music.

JIMI

I've always dreamed of making it with a Barry back-up singer. *(beat)* What are you thinking about?

MOLLY

My mother.

JIMI

I must really turn you on.

MOLLY

I was her little Barbie Doll, right? One day after Kindergarten I ran outside, ripped off this stupid prissy dress and splashed in puddles barefoot. *(Jimi laughs)* A woman walked by and said, "Who's that strange kid dancing in the mud?" My mother, who had run after me horrified, said, "I don't know." I stood there; a hair ribbon mangled at my feet, and was...erased. So...that's what I was thinking. I'm rambling. Sorry.

JIMI

Always apologizing.

MOLLY

I'm—

JIMI

(He attempts to kiss her. She pulls away) And always pulling away when I try to kiss you.

MOLLY

I don't.

JIMI

Prove it.

MOLLY

They could come back any—

JIMI

My eyes are closed and my lips ready. *(He hits a pose)* Kiss, please.

MOLLY

Jimi—

JIMI

No one will see. Not even me. *(He covers his eyes)* Kiss, please.

MOLLY

Time to go in.

JIMI

Why are you running away from me?

MOLLY

This is a party, remember? I'm going inside.

JIMI

Mol, I've never met anyone like you, who makes me laugh so hard, who...what I'm trying to say is — *(Going to her. Taking her in his arms)* You don't have to be nervous with me.

MOLLY

Let's go.

JIMI
Did you hear me? I love you. I really--

MOLLY
I'm not who you think I am.

JIMI
We'll take it slow.

MOLLY
Let's go inside.

JIMI
Look at me.

MOLLY
Let's go inside.

JIMI
Trust me.

MOLLY
Stop acting like a romantic hero!

JIMI
It's who I am.

MOLLY
I can't give you what you want!

JIMI
What do *you* want?

MOLLY

I'm scared! *(beat)* I feel...not good enough...like if I vanish everyone will breath easier or something. *(Jimi pulls her into an embrace. She cries.)*

JIMI

 I won't hurt you. I promise.

They start rocking--barely moving--in a slow dance. Jimi tenderly hums "Copacabana." After a few moments, Wings and Ty enter. Ty has whip cream all over his face and in his hair—perhaps a whip cream turban.

WINGS

Oh...sorry. Kali wants help with the cake. *(He look at Ty and starts laughing)* She says we're no good in the kitchen.

MOLLY

What'd you do?

TY

Long story.

MOLLY

(to Jimi) We better go help.

TY

(Exiting with Molly and Jimi)

I thought it was festive.

Wings is alone. He looks around to make sure he's alone. He takes off his shirt. He closes his eyes and experiences the evening. Slowly, he starts moving—he's embarking on a personal ritual—spiritual—the movement is dance-like but not dance. Wings moves to his own inner-music. Jake enters. He discovers Wings and stops, frozen by the sight. After a few moments he whispers:

JAKE

Wings? Do you want to be alone?

Wings shakes his head and continues. Jake watches until he's finished.

That was beautiful.

WINGS

(Continuing the movement)
"We are what we think; all that we are arises with our thoughts; with our thoughts we make the world."

JAKE

Great Native American Saying.

WINGS

(he stops moving) Buddha.

JAKE

I suck.

WINGS

We are what we think.

JAKE

Michael talked about all that spiritual stuff but he didn't live it. Like you.

WINGS
He lived it.

JAKE
He didn't. *(beat)* You cold?

WINGS
No.

JAKE
So.

WINGS
So.

JAKE
 I'm sorry I flipped out.

WINGS
Maybe it was a mistake to be alone after he died. We had each other but you--

JAKE
Were you pissed at me for leaving?

WINGS
I understood.

JAKE
You didn't answer the question.

WINGS
You had to deal in your own way.

JAKE
Were you pissed?

WINGS
I don't look at things that way.

JAKE
Wings, you're human. Were you pissed?

WINGS
Yes.

Beat

JAKE
Do you want my jacket?

WINGS
I'm fine.

JAKE
You're shivering.

WINGS
I want to feel the wind on my chest. I want to absorb the moon.

Beat

JAKE
What were you up to while I was gone?

WINGS
Nothing much.

JAKE
Are you seeing anyone?

WINGS
No.

JAKE
So, my buddy Wings is still a virgin.

WINGS
I jerk off. *(beat)*A lot. *(they laugh)* I did have a date last week.

JAKE
How'd that go?

WINGS
Not so good.

JAKE
What happened?

WINGS
He was a very negative person. All he talked about was how much he wished he wasn't gay.

JAKE
Sounds like a fun night.

WINGS
Too bad, too. He was cute.

JAKE
His loss.

WINGS
Thanks. Do you?

JAKE
What? Jerk off a lot?

WINGS
(laughing) No. Wake up in the morning and wish you weren't gay.

JAKE
What I wake up wishing is that our fucking country would grow up.

WINGS
Yeah.

JAKE
I mean... *(he takes WINGS' hand)* look at this hand. The veins, the palm, the fingers, like every other human hand. And unless this hand is going to hurt someone, who cares what color it is or who it wants to touch.

WINGS
Or how it prays.

JAKE
Or how it prays.

WINGS
But there's hope. A lot of people do get it.

JAKE
I know. But then I was in the store the other night and I picked up this DVD to buy. It had two guys kissing on the cover and this lady was looking at it over my shoulder. She said, "That's not a good *choice*." I said, "Oh, you've seen it?" And she repeated, "That's not a good choice." I figured out what she meant. So, I turned around and said, Desire is biological, lady. The body responds before the mind has a chance to think about it. Just like in your heterosexual reality but I doubt you've been laid in 20 years, so maybe this makes no sense at all, but obviously, AROUSAL is NOT A CHOICE. When I see a hot guy, I don't *choose* to feel desire. I don't say: "Penis, get hard, NOW!" It just happens. So, do the math: Being gay is not a choice, never was a choice, and no matter what movie I rent tonight, I will still be gay when I wake up in the morning.

WINGS
You didn't say any of that, did you?

JAKE
No. But I really wanted to. *(beat)* Do you?

WINGS
What?

JAKE
I mean, you asked for a reason. Do you?

WINGS

Do I what?

JAKE

Wish you weren't gay. Jesus! Is that what this is all about? Wings, you're fucking beautiful: inside and out. I mean, look at you—what you said--you want to feel the wind on your chest. I love that. (*Affectionately mocking*) "I want to absorb the moon"—I mean, how many people wish they could be that free?

Jake takes off his shirt and stands. He attempts Wings' ritual by imitating it. He remembers the beginning but gets stuck. Wings stands next to him and demonstrates. Jake sincerely tries to do it and fails. Wings shows him again. He fails again. Wings moves behind him and moves Jake's arms for him, helping him to discover the movement, rhythm, and feel of the gesture. It becomes sensual. Slowly, Jake gives in to Wings and allows himself to be moved like a puppet. Then, Jake's soul is opened. He is in the moment. And he melts against Wings. Eyes closed.

Pause.

WINGS

There are times I close my eyes and see myself in space: I'm floating inside the milky-way, white dust touching me, covering me like a blanket. And I hear a voice: maybe God's, maybe my mother's, maybe mine, but a soft voice says: Nothing matters but love. Nothing else matters.

They kiss.

WINGS

(*Taking Jake's hand*) Look at this beautiful hand.

Jake pulls away suddenly. He crosses and puts on his shirt. He picks up Wings' shirt and hands it to him. He sits.

WINGS
It's ok.

JAKE
I'm so confused about so many things.

WINGS
It's okay if you don't feel the same.

Jake crosses to Wings with urgency and pulls him into a long kiss.

JAKE
I hope you feel the same when you find out why I left.

KALI screams offstage and then there is group laughter. Wings puts on his shirt.

KALI (O.S.)
My hands are full. Stop groping.

TY (O.S.)
But you're so grope-able!

KALI, TY, JIMI, and MOLLY enter with the cake, knife, paper plates, and forks.

KALI
(to Jake) I'm pissed at you.

TY

(Crossing to Jake , speaking to Kali.)

O, his offense is rank; it smells to heaven.
What if this cursed hand *(He lifts Jake's arm)*
Were thicker than itself with brother's blood?
Is there not rain in heaven to wash it white as snow?

JAKE

I'm sorry I freaked out.

KALI

Forgiven. Sit your fat asses down for some cake.

JAKE

Where's Liz?

KALI

Looking for you.

MOLLY

Don't cut yourself with that thing.

KALI

If I do remember to tell the doctor I'm allergic to penicillin.

JIMI

(Playing the game he's learned)
You're not allergic to penicillin.

(They all just look at him.)

TY
Yes, she is.

JIMI
I feel stupid. Do I look stupid?

KALI/TY/MOLLY
You're not stupid.

Kali passes out cake.

KALI
Guest's first.

JIMI
Thanks. You're fast.

KALI

(Handing Molly a plate.)
I'm a trained professional.

MOLLY
Thanks.

KALI
Hey, anybody else notice Mol hasn't said "I'm sorry" in like 20 minutes?

TY
Bravo!

She hands a plate to Jake but just as he reaches for it, she pulls it away.

KALI
More sugar for you is a bad idea.

JAKE
I thought you'd like the drama.

KALI
More drama I could do without because last night *I flipped out!* There was this guy and his mousy girlfriend in my section, right, and he starts yelling for his check--all the way across the dining room. I walk over, hand him the check, and very sweetly say, "I'm sorry. I'm rather busy. Thanks for your patience." He holds the check up in front of my face and rips it in half.

MOLLY
No.

KALI
Very calm, I place a second one on the table. "Hey, *girlie*," he says,--I smile, suppressing the urge to dump the very hot coffee in my hand all over his crotch--"warn me before you start working in the real world." Can you believe it? I've paid my dues. I'm a good person. I was about to look him in the eye and say: "I'm a struggling artist, pal. I'm enlightened you moron." But then I looked down and saw a big soup stain on my skirt. I went to the bathroom to wash it off and came back determined to reclaim my dignity. I probably would have too if I hadn't come out with my skirt tucked up in my underwear.

MOLLY
And the jerk gets away thinking he's done nothing wrong.

JIMI

Ready to treat the next woman he meets like crap.

TY

Yeah, but he totally screwed his karma. He'll never meet the woman of his dreams by treating mine like shit. *(Beat. Molly is looking at him with wonderment)* What?

KALI

Don't be stunned, Mol. That was the beer talking.

TY

That was me talking. That guy sucks and you're the most amazing woman on the planet. (to Molly) No offense. *(He gets on one knee and addresses Kail)* "But soft, what light through yonder window breaks?"

KALI.

I love you, too.

MOLLY

What're you doing Wings?

WINGS

(Holding up one of the candles and staring into it)

There was a time when candles were the only source of light. I bet people held them up like gods, adored them, even prayed for stillness so no wind would blow them out.

MOLLY

Wings is very happy tonight.

WINGS
Wings is very happy tonight, yes.

KALI
Why is everyone talking in third person?

TY
Ty isn't.

LIZ enters

KALI
(handing her a plate) Just in time!

TY
(mouth full) This is great.

KALI
Stop eating! Everyone! We forgot candles and singing!

She goes to a bag and pulls out a candle. During the following she puts it on LIZ' piece of cake and attempts to light it.

LIZ
It doesn't matter.

KALI
Of course it matters! You're legal tonight!

LIZ
I'm serious. Don't.

KALI

Stop moving or I'll burn your face off. *(She gets it lit)* There. Now, everyone!

TY, Molly, Kali, and Jimi start singing Happy Birthday. Kali notices Jake isn't singing.

I said everyone!

(Kali crosses to Jake)

SING DAMNIT!

Everyone stops. Kali crosses and blows LIZ's candle out

KALI

That's it. I'm done trying. I don't know what the hell's going on here but I. Am. Done. *(She starts cleaning up the cake mess)*

TY

(to LIZ) Why are you being such a bitch, tonight?

KALI

Don't, Ty.

TY

She's tried to give you the perfect party and—

LIZ

I'm not in the mood for one of your rants.

TY

This isn't a rant. You hurt her feelings, Liz!

LIZ

I never asked for this party. I wanted to spend the night alone.

KALI

Thanks.

LIZ

Kal, I appreciate it, I do, but—

KALI

I'm going in.

JAKE

Don't go. There's something I need to say.

LIZ

Let's clean up. We should do these dishes.

(She starts collecting them.)

TY

They're plastic.

LIZ

We recycle.

JAKE

It's time you all knew.

MOLLY

Knew what?

LIZ
Don't do this.

JAKE
The truth.

KALI
About what?

LIZ
Don't do this!

TY
What are you two--

JAKE.
This is about Michael.

LIZ
I mean it!

MOLLY
What about him?

TY
What 're you guys talking about?

LIZ
I'll never speak to you again!

JAKE
How he--

LIZ
Jake!

Jake grabs her by the arms. The plates fall to the ground.

JAKE
Is that what you want? Is that what you really want?

LIZ
Stop it!

JAKE
I'm tired of this.

LIZ
Let go.

JAKE
This is important to me.

LIZ
To you and no one else.

JAKE
It's time!

LIZ
Fine! *(even)* Go ahead. Throw up your guilt in a big, smelly heap. Stink up the air with your conscience, make everybody sick. Just remember: You no longer exist for me.

KALI

What the hell is going on?

JAKE

You really mean that? *(LIZ crosses down left and sits.)* I didn't want it to be this way.

TY

What's going on?

KALI

Say it.

JAKE

There are two things. First, you need to know....*(He looks at Liz)*...Liz? *(She ignores him)* Michael and I were lovers.

TY

What?

JAKE.

We couldn't tell you because we didn't want to hurt Liz. We didn't mean for it to happen—it just....did.

TY

He was gay? He lied to us?

JAKE

Yes. No. He loved Liz, he did, but he was confused and--

KALI

How could you do that to her?
Kali goes to LIZ

TY

How long did you screw around behind our backs?

JAKE

It started on that camping trip.

TY

The camping trip? He was with Liz until he died. That's months, man!

KALI

This sucks, Jake. This really sucks.

JAKE

Let me explain! Please! On the first night of the trip Michael and I couldn't sleep, so we took a walk through the woods and discovered this cove with a small pond in the middle. I realized at that moment we had never been alone together. I also realized...I was in love with him. I loved his sense of adventure; I loved his weird obsessions with dumb things; I loved the way he could make you feel special with that stupid wink of his. *(beat)* It was muggy that night. We took off our shirts and let the water move up our legs, trying to cool off. We were sitting so close...I could smell his breath. And it was like his breath was pulling me close to him and I laid my head on his shoulder. I thought, what did I just do, you know, like he's going to freak out and our friendship will never be the same. I couldn't believe I risked that so I sat up fast and mumbled something like, "Sorry, kind of tired." We didn't move for a long time. Then, he looked out over the pond and said, "Can I kiss you?" I was scared so I said no. But, then...under the water, our feet touched and that was it—we fell into each other and somewhere in the middle of it all I realized I was crying because I was alive for the first time—he was *making* me alive for the first time-- and I knew that this is what people talked about, wrote about, made movies about. God, it was...it *was* God, speaking through us.

TY
Well, so much for honesty, you mother fucker.

JAKE
Ty.

TY
This renders everything false, man! REASSESSMENT!

JAKE
There's more!

TY
I don't want to hear anymore! RE-A-SSESSMENT!

JAKE
Michael's dad caught us together.

MOLLY
Oh my god.

JAKE
His parents went to a convention out of town so we stayed at his house. His mom got sick, they came home early, his dad walked in on us. Saw us naked in bed. He didn't say a word. Just closed the door. I jumped out the window and ran back to the dorm.

WINGS
What happened?

JAKE

Michael called me later. He was a mess. At breakfast his dad told him to pack his stuff and get out of the house. He said he never wanted to see his faggot son again, didn't care where he went, and to forget about med. school. He was freaking out so I told him to meet me at the dorm and we'd figure something out. He never showed up. Six hours I waited and nothing. So I call Liz. I tell her everything. After all those months of hiding I just had to get it out. I was scared, she was hurt but we had to find Michael so we searched everywhere: library, train station, hospitals, hotels—finally, it hits me: " I know exactly where he is!" We drove out to the campsite. We ran into the woods, out to the cove, and there he was. But... he wasn't breathing. He was just lying there in the grass...not breathing.

MOLLY

Oh, my god...

JAKE

The thing is...there was no hemorrhage. His father made it up.

KALI

What're you talking about?

JAKE

His image. His social standing. That's what I'm talking about. They told the media Michael died of a hemorrhage to protect the goddamn family image. In the grass...next to him...we found an empty pill bottle.

LONG PAUSE

We wanted you to remember him like he was. In a way, we were no better than his parents.

Without warning, Kali vehemently throws one of the flowerpots onto the ground. It shatters. She picks up a second, throws it, and laughs maniacally. She finds a third but Jake grabs her arms in mid-air.

JAKE
Stop it.

KALI
Let go!

JAKE.
Come on.

KALI
HOW DARE YOU!

She pulls away. The pot falls and shatters. She bends down to retrieve the pieces.

JAKE
You'll hurt yourself.

KALI
Don't touch me.

JAKE
It was a blurry mess, Kal.

KALI
You were worse than his parents. They kept us from his funeral. You kept us from his life.

JAKE
You're not--

KALI
What a farce! We called ourselves family and the one time we needed each other most you two decide to play hero!

JAKE
That's what I'm--

MOLLY
God! We sat in that circle the night of his funeral and decided—*together*—that we would drop out of school because "life was so random." But it wasn't. It was an act of *free will*. Michael's *choice*. And we—oh, my god—

TY
Wiped away, man. Wiped- A-Way.
JAKE
What?

TY
The last five months—the last two years-- who's Michael? I don't know him. He betrayed us. You betrayed us. One big construction of deceit!

JAKE
This is what I figured out in Colorado--

TY
Unbelievable!

JAKE

In Colorado—

KALI

Enough is enough!

JAKE

SHUT-UP AND LISTEN! I realized that I
may not have taken pills but I was running scared too, like Michael.
All of us are--

LIZ

We did what we had to do.

JAKE

We did what we *decided* to do. This isn't about *what* happened anymore,
it's about *what's not happening now. (to Kali)* Ask yourself. Who's really
holding you back? *(to the others)* Who? Michael glorified those stars for
falling but I say falling's too easy! *(pointing at the stars)* I admire you and
you and you and you and you *(arms open to the heavens)* every one of you
that hangs on and keeps fighting!

LIZ

(To Jake)
Look how great everyone feels. Proud of yourself?

JAKE

You're not listening.

LIZ

You come in here with your righteous "need to confess," to unburden
yourself, and expect everyone to get runny with forgiveness.

JAKE
I'm talking about what it takes to live an honest life. If you want to run away from that don't blame me thirty years from now.

LIZ
You're so arrogant!

JAKE.
And you're so scared, Lizzie.

LIZ
Shut-up.

JAKE
Scared of wanting too much.

LIZ
Stop talking!

JAKE
Of what? Being hurt again?

LIZ
Stop talking! *(She pounds his chest)* Stop, stop, stop, stop, stop, stop*(the anger becomes anguish as she makes a profound realization)*....oh my, god.... oh, my god...*(She slides down him to the ground. PAUSE.)*...I am a coward.

JAKE
                    (Moving down to her.)
No, you're scared. They're two different things. But we can't let the fear win. *(He slowly looks up from Liz and sees the group staring at him. He starts to break.)* We did the wrong thing. I'm sorry. We wanted....we just...

87

He's sobbing now. After a moment, Wings moves down to them both and wraps his arms around them.
Then, Jimi crosses down to Jake, takes the bracelet off his wrist, and puts it on Jake's.)

JIMI
A gift.

JAKE
Why?

JIMI
I'll tell you later.

Ty crosses to leave.

KALI
Where are you going?

TY
I don't know. Home, New York, Afghanistan.

KALI
Don't go.

JAKE
Ty, stay.

TY
You betrayed us.

JAKE
I know.

TY
You're an asshole.

JAKE
I know.

Liz crosses to Ty

LIZ
If you leave, you'll regret it the rest of your life. Trust me. I know how that feels tonight. We can start over.

Ty regards her. Then, he crosses and sits next to Kali. She takes his hand.

KALI
                              (To Ty)
I know: Tomorrow seems very far away.

(Silence. Stillness.)

MOLLY
Can someone tell me how I'm supposed to feel? I don't know what to feel.

WINGS
Look at the sky.

Take a deep breath.
And feel what a gift it is to simply be here.

They experience the moment.

Lights slowly fade.

End of Play

33879000R00057

Made in the USA
Charleston, SC
25 September 2014